The Everyday, Anytime
Guide to
Christian
LEADERSHIP

The Everyday, Anytime Guide to Christian LEADERSHIP

Walt Kallestad

Augsburg
MINNEAPOLIS

$7/_{95}$

THE EVERYDAY, ANYTIME GUIDE TO CHRISTIAN LEADERSHIP

Cover design: Cindy Cobb-Olson
Inside design: Kathy McEnaney
Cartoon illustrations: John Bush

Library of Congress Cataloging in Publication Data

Kallestad, Walther P., 1948–
    The everyday, anytime guide to Christian leadership/Walt Kallestad.
        p.   cm.
    ISBN 0-8066-2723-9 :
    1. Christian leadership.   I. Title
    BV652.1.K355   1994
    262'.1—dc20   94-2151
                                                                    CIP

The paper used in this publication meets the minimum requirements of American National Standard for Information Sciences—Permanence of Paper for Printed Library Materials, ANSI Z329.48-1984. ∞™

Manufactured in the U.S.A.   AF 10-27239

98   97   96   95   94   1   2   3   4   5   6   7   8   9   10

Contents

Foreword

Through the years many books on leadership have been published, and most have ended up on shelves in executive offices. Rarely is a leadership book written for ordinary folk, regardless of their positions or authority. *The Everyday, Anytime Guide to Christian Leadership* is a book for you, regardless of when and where you may find yourself leading. It provides a wonderful opportunity to learn about the real character of leadership from someone who models what he teaches.

Walt Kallestad is a leader who has a following. He is the kind of person people choose to follow because he demonstrates a commitment to excellence and to the future. Walt Kallestad is an outstanding visionary leader in today's church.

Kallestad delightfully blends personal experience and reflection to describe the character of a Christian leader. He provides a sensitive, balanced set of leadership principles and concrete, realistic, practical suggestions for being a leader. The writing style is easy to read and understand. You will find in this book both amusement and content on which to reflect. But most importantly, you will be motivated and challenged to live the principles that shape the character of a leader.

So read on—today, every day, and anytime you want a humorous, flexible, and religious perspective on living as a leader.

ROBERT H. SCHULLER

Acknowledgments

Leadership Is Influence is the caption under a picture I have hanging on my office wall. My life has been positively influenced in many ways by my beloved parents, Walther and Florence Kallestad, my wonderful wife, Mary, my children, and other family members and friends. I am thankful for those supportive relationships. I also thank God daily for others along the way—work associates, teachers, and friends—who have had an influence in shaping my life as a leader in the church today.

Others deserving significant thanks are my leadership mentors—Lyle Schaller, Robert H. Schuller, Lloyd Ogilvie, and Norman Vincent Peale. These giants have enabled me to see farther than I imagined possible by letting me stand on their shoulders.

In the development of this book I have had some wonderful partners whom I wish to acknowledge. Rose Jackson has made a significant contribution as my research team leader. I also appreciate the work of my editor, John Kober, and the other quality team members at Augsburg Fortress Publishers.

Finally, my greatest thank-you belongs to the greatest leader who ever walked the face of the earth—Jesus Christ. It is to Jesus Christ and the proclamation of the gospel that I dedicate this book.

Introduction

EFFICIENCY:
Getting the job done right.

EFFECTIVENESS:
Getting the right job done.

EXCELLENCE:
Getting the right job done right.

Leaders take the lead

Definition of a leader (in mountaineering): Being the first person to ascend a pitch without the security of a rope above you.[1]

A leader should always provide protection when climbing so that, if those following should slip, they will not be endangered.

No matter how you choose to measure success, leadership is a key ingredient to being successful. In mountaineering, the lives of all the climbers may depend on it. Churches without it drift aimlessly, and nations have fallen for lack of it. Effective leadership is a key to success in all of life.

Our world faces a leadership crisis—in government, business, education, church, and every other sector of society, both public and private. Many people see the crisis as a problem, but it also can be interpreted as an opportunity. Seen as an opportunity, a crisis is a gift to help us find new and better ways to develop dynamic, effective leaders.

[1]Walker, Kevin. *Learn Rock Climbing in a Weekend* (London: Dorling Kindersley Limited, 1991).

Recently I had the opportunity to visit with the archbishop of Finland. In our conversation we discovered that we both shared a genuine concern about a lack of dynamic leadership worldwide. That same concern has been echoed by others, including bishops, seminary officials, political leaders, international business leaders, and university presidents. The fact is that without leaders who can relate well to other people and to the issues around them, our future will not be as magnificent as God imagined it to be.

The following story illustrates where we sometimes find ourselves in the church when it comes to recognizing the need for effective leadership. A minister was recently interviewing for the senior pastor position of a 25-year-old congregation. The minister worked hard to impress the interview committee. The ministerial candidate said, "If I am chosen to be the senior minister of this church, I promise to lead this church into the 20th century."

One of the committee members corrected him by saying, "You must mean the 21st century."

The minister asserted, "Oh, no; I mean the 20th century. We must take only one century at a time."

The point of the story is that we have a long way to go to efficiently, effectively, and excellently carry out successful 21st-century mission. And we all must be concerned about leadership because we all are leaders at some time in some area of our lives. I am convinced that successful 21st-century leadership will require developing and deploying leaders who:

LOVE UNCONDITIONALLY
ENVISION THE FUTURE EXCEPTIONALLY
AFFIRM CONTINUOUSLY
DISCIPLINE WITH DETERMINATION
ENERGIZE OTHERS ENTHUSIASTICALLY
RISK BOLDLY
SERVE SELFLESSLY
HOPE RELENTLESSLY
IMAGINE IMMEASURABLY
PRAY PERSISTENTLY

Be practical, make it relevant, insist on being user friendly, target ordinary folk, use common sense—these were the principles that guided the writing of this book. We can learn about leadership theory and process from more academic treatments of the subject. But from a practical standpoint, leadership that works needs to be sufficiently simple. Leadership is a lifestyle, and this book will help assimilate leading with daily living. Together let's explore and exercise the possibilities of this kind of leadership.

Chapter 1

Love Unconditionally

———◆———

Love the Lord your God with all your heart and with all your soul and with all your mind. This is the first and greatest commandment. And the second is like it: Love your neighbor as yourself.

Matthew 22:37-39 NIV

1

"*T*wo teams," said the master, "went up to the mountain to climb. The leaders were equally matched in strength. The leader of the first team instructed his team members to rope up. 'Though the climbing here is easy, you never know when we will run into ice,' he cautioned, and he tied himself in with the team. The second team roped up as well, and both teams began their climb.

"After some time they came to a glacier and, not much farther along the river of ice, to a chasm a little less than ten feet wide. 'It would be easy enough to jump,' said the leader of the second team, 'if not for our ropes.'

" 'No,' countered the leader of the first team. 'Not everyone on my team is as strong as I. I think I can make it across, but we will stay roped together to anchor each other on the jump.'

"So saying, he nodded to the rest of his team. They braced their feet in the snow and held the ropes firmly. The leader looked intently at the far edge as he ran toward the chasm and pushed off, landing on the other side breathless but safe. He turned and braced himself as the second on his team followed, landing precariously close to the rim. Each team member followed in turn until all were safely across.

"Shaking his head, the leader of the second team asserted, 'I know I can do it more easily without the weight of ropes.' He freed himself from the ropes, backed off a few paces and ran forward, launching himself over the chasm, landing with inches to spare. 'See,' he said, 'it is easy!' The second member of his team likewise untied himself and, more laboriously, began to huff and run across the ice field. Hurling himself from the rim, his body arched into space; then somehow he seemed to lose momentum, and his ice axe hacked uselessly at the crumbling far rim of the chasm. He fell in a heap to a ledge some 20 feet below the lip of the chasm.

"Now who," the master asked, "was the true leader?"

"The one who stayed roped to his team," the disciple replied.

"And **love** is the rope," said the master.

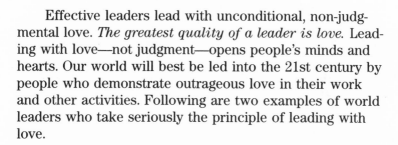

Effective leaders lead with unconditional, non-judgmental love. *The greatest quality of a leader is love.* Leading with love—not judgment—opens people's minds and hearts. Our world will best be led into the 21st century by people who demonstrate outrageous love in their work and other activities. Following are two examples of world leaders who take seriously the principle of leading with love.

During a recent speaking tour of mine through Europe, the president and CEO of one of the world's largest banks came up and introduced himself to me. During our conversation I asked him what the secret was to his success. He shared with me that the key to his super success as a leader was *love*. He went on to explain that every negotiated contract, every loan, every decision was defined by love. Genuine concern for the customer and for her or his needs was more than just a principle of good business.

Jan Carlzon, chairman and CEO of Scandinavian Airlines, speaks from his experience when he suggests that there are two great motivators in life. One is fear. The other is love. You can lead an organization by fear, but if you do, you will ensure that people won't perform up to their real capabilities.

Both of these leaders have decided that there is great power in love, and they have chosen to lead with love. As Christian leaders, our model for such love was best demonstrated by the greatest leader who ever lived—Jesus Christ. The principle that guided his leadership is summed up in the words of Matthew 22:37-39 (see page 15).

Effective leadership begins with God's gracious love for us and our wholehearted love for God. Such love aligns the mind, heart, spirit, and everything else with God's designs and desires, rather like the way an orchestra tunes up to the "A" of the principal violin. When you let God work through you, your leadership will be constructive and will please God. Without love for God, leadership can quickly become destructive. The world has destructive leaders. They are the ones, like Saddam Hussein during the 1992 Gulf War, who are motivated by hate and retaliatory unforgiveness. The absence of love is obvious in destructive leadership. Constructive leaders know there is no substitute for love and forgiveness.

Effective leaders who lead with love are the first to forgive and forget. Many years ago, a businessman came to me for counseling. He said his problem was that whenever he had a fight with his boss, she became historical. I interrupted him and said, "You mean hysterical."

"No," he said, "I mean historical. She brings up everything I have done wrong in the past and uses it against me."

The boss needed to learn how to forgive and forget. God promises, "I will forgive and remember your sins no more" (Hebrews 8:12, paraphrased). God tells us to do the same for one another.

Great leaders know that trying to get even with someone who has hurt them isn't being constructive; it is destructive, negative leadership. Shortly after I became pastor of Community Church of Joy, a member who was upset with me said many unkind, untrue things about me. He organized private meetings in an attempt to get rid of me. I could have chosen to hurt him, too. However, my decision was not to retaliate. I chose the course of love.

Love is always a conscious decision. Loving unconditionally isn't always easy. Nevertheless, I have made the decision that unconditional love is always the *only option.* This kind of love influences the attitudes and actions of people positively. Whatever the size of your church, love impacts the way in which people relate to each other and respond to God's Word. Ultimately, at Community Church of Joy, love is one of the factors that has helped transform a 252-member church of 15 years ago into a 7,000-member church today.

Loving leadership doesn't ignore problems or overlook prejudice. It does face them head-on with love that is tough enough to deal with difficult problems and unreasonable people. It is best described in the Bible in these words:

> If I speak in tongues of mortals and of angels, but do not have love, I am a noisy gong or a clanging cymbal. And if I have prophetic powers, and understand all mysteries and all knowledge, and if I have all faith, so as to remove mountains, but do not have love, I am nothing. If I give away all my possessions, and if I hand over my body so that I may boast, but do not have love, I gain nothing.
> Love is patient; love is kind; love is not envious or boastful or arrogant or rude. It does not insist on its own way; it is not irritable or resentful; it does not rejoice in wrongdoing, but rejoices in the truth. It bears all things, believes all things, hopes all things, endures all things.
> Love never ends.
>
> 1 Corinthians 13:1-8a NRSV

Love is the essence of the character of a leader. Dr. Frank Harrington, in a message to his church, Peachtree

Presbyterian in Atlanta, Georgia, told the story of love-filled leadership. To him, the emotional peak of a recent summer Olympics was not when one of the athletes won a gold medal. It was when an act of love was played out in one of the events. Perhaps you saw it. Derek Redmon, a British runner, tore his hamstring muscle during the 400-meter race. But he continued the race. His face was wrenched with pain, and it was painful to watch him hobble and lurch down the track. It was obvious to the spectators that he had no intention of stopping. He was determined to finish! Most people forgot who won or lost that 400-meter race, because they shared that young man's struggle as he hobbled along in pain. Just when he seemed on the verge of collapse and could run no farther, a man appeared out of the stands. It was his father. He waved aside the security people and put his arms around that boy and supported him until *together* they crossed the finish line. It was love that did that! The father's action is a strong picture of how God loves, supports, and helps us in our struggles and trials. It is God's love that does that.

A loving leader lifts up those who are hurting and runs with them until they achieve their victory. An effective leader is roped to the team with unconditional love and holds fast until they cross the chasm. This is the kind of love that is essential for effective 21st-century leadership.

Leadership workout

Practice loving unconditionally with these suggestions:

Look for excuses to be the first to forgive and forget.

Optimize each other's worth whenever you speak.

Vocalize affirmation through daily compliments.

Express unlimited grace by making mistakes on the side of love, not judgment.

Effective leadership requires extravagant love, as well as the commitment to

ENVISION THE FUTURE EXCEPTIONALLY!

Chapter 2

Envision the Future Exceptionally

———◆———

The one who sees not beyond today must simply let it be.

The one who envisions tomorrow is the one who will <u>make</u> it be.

2

"*T*wo people," said the master, "went walking, each on a journey through the forest. One had a destination, a map, and a compass. The other had in mind only a pleasant walk. As the day passed and the shadows lengthened, they began to think of finding the edge of the forest and their destinations.

"The first, lacking a compass or map, said, 'Just ahead is a mighty tree. From there, perhaps, I can see the way out of the forest.' Walking to the tree and seeing no clear direction, the traveler looked toward another tree that was not far away. That looked like an even stronger tree, and he was sure that it must be near the edge of the forest. From there he could surely find the way. But that tree gave no clue, either, to the way to the edge of the forest. Seeing many more sturdy trunks in the gathering twilight, the traveler reasoned, 'If I go from tree to tree, surely I must find my way out of the forest at last.' So the traveler wandered and wandered until darkness descended.

"The second traveler also noted the gathering twilight. From her bag this traveler pulled a map and compass. Aligning the map with the compass, and taking a bearing from a rocky outcropping she could see through the trees, she set herself to walking true north, the way that would take her out of the forest, past the encompassing trees, and to her evening's destination. And at length she found herself on the edge of the forest and on the road to her destination.

"Now which traveler," asked the master, "would reach the destination? And which would you rather follow into another forest?"

"The second traveler," replied the disciple. "The first traveler's eyes were only on the trees before him, but the second had her eyes on the destination. Because she saw the destination, she was prepared with a plan to reach it."

———————◆———————

Effective leaders envision the future exceptionally. They are able to stay ahead of tomorrow. A Bible verse worth remembering is: "Where there is no vision, the people perish" (Proverbs 29:18 KJV).

A short time ago I delivered four lectures at St. Nicholas Church in Strasbourg, France. In this church it is believed that John Calvin was a minister, Martin Luther preached, and Albert Schweitzer was the music minister. Wow—what a lineup! There had been people of great vision in this church, yet only five centuries after they opened, the church doors were locked. No one came any longer; only pigeons ever saw the inside. How did that happen? It happened because the vision or purpose for the church was lost. Without a vision, the church literally perished.

In 1992, the local bishop invited any pastor who was interested to submit a vision for this empty, historic church building. One pastor was equal to the challenge. He stayed up all night writing down his vision. He submitted it to the bishop, who eventually granted permission for the pastor to carry out his vision. When I spoke later in that church, I was excited to see 300 to 400 people crammed into the building. Today that church has the largest attendance of any Lutheran church in France. With a vision, people prosper—without a vision, people perish.

Empty churches do not please God. We are not called to simply build churches—we are called to fill them.

Churches the world over have lost their vision. That is the reason thousands of churches will be closed before the year 2000. A recent church study discovered evidence that, in the United States, 700 people a day are leaving Christian churches, and 100,000 U.S. churches will close by the year 2000. There are beautiful cathedrals all over the world with only a handful of people worshiping inside. The saying in boldface above is attributed to St. Augustine. It is a good summary of the problem and our call to address it.

WHAT WE SEE IS WHAT WILL BE

Alive, dynamic churches require a vision that looks beyond the immediate issues, circumstances, problems, and even successes. Some time ago I spoke at a conference in Syracuse, New York. Before leaving Syracuse, I visited a museum that told about the history of the area. Some early settlers there saw only the marshy land, but one local leader envisioned a great city. That's why, decades later, Syracuse has become a great city. When I arrived as the new pastor, Community Church of Joy was only a handful of people, yet I saw a church of thousands. What I saw is what came to be.

Making a vision reality requires enormous energy and effort. But you need to start with a vision so you can put today's work into proper perspective and align your life and mission to achieve maximum results. Fifteen years ago, I was overwhelmed by the daily responsibilities and demands as pastor of Community Church of Joy. (Such a feeling is not unusual among clergy and others in positions of responsibility.) I worked 15 hours a day, and I couldn't imagine working any harder. It was impossible to accomplish everything each day; working on the future seemed only a dream. However, I often listened to leaders talk about how essential it was to work today on tomorrow.

Wrestling with this dilemma, I made the commitment to develop a weekly "dream day." Every Friday now, I have a dream day when the only work I do is work on the future. I set aside the past and present unfinished work on top of my desk, and I focus on the next week, or upcoming month, or following year, or future decade. This dream day relieves present pressures and stress. I can catch a glimpse of how what I am investing my time, talents, and treasures in *today* is going to pay off one, three, five, or ten years from now. This creates in me new, invigorating energy, endurance, and enthusiasm to *keep on keeping on.*

Vision helps leaders see what's coming next. Wayne Gretzky was asked why he was the world's greatest hockey player. He replied that, while most hockey players go where the hockey puck *is*, he always goes where the puck *will be*. By seeing tomorrow *today*, we can anticipate and avoid many future problems and pitfalls. When all our resources go into problem solving, we become worn out, unproductive, and unfulfilled. Leadership that looks ahead can see problems coming and can make the necessary adjustments to avoid many problems. Problem *avoidance* is much more productive than problem *solving*; it enables us to accomplish more and become more effective leaders.

A great story tells about a southern gentleman enjoying an afternoon drive in the country. The weather was perfect, so he opened all the car windows to enjoy the fresh air. Suddenly a fancy sports car came flying along the curving road from the opposite direction, the driver apparently trying to regain control of the vehicle. As the two cars passed, the driver of the sports car yelled out, *"Pig!"* This instantly angered the suave southern gentleman, since he was driving the speed limit and *not* the one losing control of his vehicle.

Before the sports car got out of earshot, he stuck his head out the window and hollered back as loudly as he could, *"Sow!"* Feeling pretty good about his quick retort, he rounded the curve and ran right into a pig standing in the middle of the road. The southern gentleman could have avoided the pig problem if he had understood and heeded the other driver's warning of what was waiting for him around the next corner. Vision gives us a better grasp on the future. Better prepared leaders make tomorrow the best it can be.

One of the first things I did as the new pastor of my church was write a "1-3-5-10-year plan." With God working through me and others in the church, this blueprint for the future guided us from 252 members to more than 3,000 during the first 10 years. It helped guide us from an income of $40,000 a year to an annual income of $1,000,000. Now, as we continue to seek to do God's will and work on the future, we are making preparations to be a more effective mission-driven church. We can envision a membership of 28,000 and a yearly income of 10 to 20 million dollars. In order for that to happen, it is essential that the leadership rely on God's help to

> **ENVISION** a vision that
> **EVOLVES** into a detailed plan
> **EQUIPPING** us to implement an
> **EMPOWERING** strategy.

THE FUTURE WILL BE WHAT YOU ENVISION IT TO BE

Whatever the size of your church or job or family, after the vision is shaped, people will be shaped by that vision. Great leaders know this. They are, therefore, people who shape their vision creatively and confidently. People like Walt Disney, Henry Ford, Thomas Edison, Mother Teresa, Margaret Thatcher, Martin Luther King Jr., and numerous others were themselves shaped by the way they envisioned the future. Such is the power of vision. This power is a gift from God. God is greatly complimented when we envision what God envisions for us. May our prayer today be this:

God, take my mind and think through it.
Take my imagination and flow through it.
Take my vision and help me grow
through it.
Help me to envision the future as
exceptionally as you do.

Leadership workout

Practice envisioning the future exceptionally with these
suggestions:

Expand your horizons by stretching your imagination.

Nurture new ideas.

Vote for positive changes, with a welcoming attitude.

Imagine the impossible.

Stay ahead of tomorrow.

Invent the future.

Operate expectantly.

Notice unlimited opportunity.

An effective leader loves unconditionally and envisions the future exceptionally. Now we will discover how important it is to take the next step, which is to

AFFIRM CONTINUOUSLY!

Chapter 3

Affirm Continuously

---◆---

AFFIRMATION leads to
   —*appreciation*
   —*aspiration*
   —*transformation*
   —*celebration*

3

"*L*isten," said the master, "to the desert night. Do you hear the sound of frogs?"

The disciple leaned forward, intently listening to the twitterings, hums, buzzes, and chirps that filled the darkness. Suddenly he straightened up. "Yes," he said, "I do hear frogs croaking."

"Does that surprise you—frogs in the desert?" the master asked.

"I'd never thought of it before, but, yes, it does," remarked the disciple. "Frogs need water, don't they? How do they survive here?"

"Water is essential to frogs, even to frogs in the desert," answered the master. "A frog's skin is porous, and must be kept moist to prevent dehydration. Here in the desert, the only way for the frog to survive is to burrow down into the ground and remain there until it hears the sound of rain upon the ground above. That may mean the frog emerges for only the few weeks of the year when rain comes to the desert. In those few weeks the frogs mate and lay eggs in the scattered pools formed by the rains. The young frogs then go from eggs to adults. In those few weeks, the frog becomes what it was meant to be. All this in response to the sound of rain."

"You could say that rain transforms the frogs," said the disciple.

"Yes, rain brings the transformation," agreed the master. "In that way, encouragement is like rain in the desert. It arouses those who lay dormant in indifference, weariness, or despair. It is the sound of affirmation, energizing them to become what they were meant to be."

The master and the disciple paused again to listen to the chorus of joyous chirps and croaks that punctuated the night.

"Encouragement brings celebration," the master smiled. "It is the affirmation that transforms, from lifelessness to life."

It is often said that great things can happen if you don't care who gets the credit. That's not totally true. It is more accurate to say that *great things can happen when you give others the credit.* Crediting people through continual affirmation is a key to effective leadership.

Effective leaders always look for ways to say thank you. Billy Graham looks for at least seven new ways to say thank you to people who have helped him financially. This has enhanced his ministry tremendously over the past 50 years. I have a friend in San Antonio, Texas, who writes notes of affirmation to people all over the world every day. He believes in leading with continuous affirmation.

In the outstanding book *In Search of Excellence* (Warner Books, 1988), Tom Peters emphasizes the importance of trying to catch someone doing something good, and then complimenting him or her enthusiastically. This generates greater productivity—*affirmation produces morale building appreciation, that produces empowering aspiration.* Recently I observed a first-time visitor to church receive a royal welcome from a public relations volunteer. I immediately told this volunteer what a tremendous job she was doing. I followed up with a thank-you note. That affirmation will have a positive influence on how she treats the next visitor. The value of affirmation is incalculable.

Affirmation builds a greater sense of worth and value in one another. My cousin discovered this firsthand. She was born with a deformed lip. Her speech was garbled and her teeth were gnarled. As a little girl, she was ashamed of how she looked and ashamed of who she was. During recess at school she would often stand far away from her classmates, hoping she wouldn't be noticed. When she walked around, she kept her head down in embarrassment. One day her well-loved grade school teacher knelt down beside her desk, lovingly looked into her eyes, and said, "You are very special. I wish you were my little girl." In that moment of affirmation, a little girl who didn't love herself at all was totally transformed. If her teacher thought she was special and wanted her, she decided that she must be of value.

Affirmation produces transformation. If you're traveling abroad, an electrical transformer is indispensable. The transformer plugs into a power source and steps the voltage up or down to provide the power necessary for an appliance to work effectively. In human terms, a transformer provides a steady source of encouragement and affirmation, empowering people to work effectively even in new, difficult, or challenging situations. Leading by affirmation is transformational leadership. The job gets done, but the greatest reward is that there is wonderful enjoyment and fulfillment in the process. When so much of the world *works to keep going*, the effective leader knows how important it is that people *keep going at work.* A paycheck doesn't bring the greatest satisfaction; appreciation does.

Affirmation builds up and brings out the best in people. In *In Search of Excellence*, Peters points out that companies achieving the most success are the companies that are able to unlock people's greatest potential. And what unlocks people's potential is continual, genuine affirmation.

A leader needs to affirm regularly, generously, genuinely, and intentionally. It is very easy to become consumed with projects and programs and forget about *people.* An effective leader knows that people are always the priority. When leaders forget that they are first and foremost in the people business, they are soon out of business.

Mary Kay Ash, the founder of Mary Kay cosmetics, enthusiastically encourages all her salespeople to pretend that everyone they meet has a sign around his or her neck that reads, "Make me feel important." She believes this is not only the key to success in sales, it is the key to success in all of life.

Affirmation produces celebration: joy in the process, pride in the finished product, and anticipation in the prospect of new challenges.

Leadership workout

Practice affirming others with these suggestions:

1. Listen carefully with your heart as well as your head.

2. Take time to dream together.

3. Send a handwritten note of appreciation.

4. Leave a message of thanks on voice mail or answering machine.

5. Send a birthday or anniversary card.

6. Say "thank you" or "I appreciate you" regularly.

7. Buy lunch or dinner to convey gratitude.

8. Give a small gift of thanks.

9. Publicly compliment excellence.

10. Offer extra time off from work to someone going the extra mile.

11. Add your own suggestions.

An effective leader combines the first three essential ingredients—(1) loving unconditionally, (2) envisioning the future exceptionally, and (3) affirming continually—with

DISCIPLINING WITH DETERMINATION!

Chapter 4

Discipline with Determination

Two Theories of Life
1. Don't Sweat the Small Stuff
Corollary: Everything is small stuff

2. Sweat the Small Stuff, and the Big Stuff
Will Take Care of Itself

Great Stuff Theory
Some small stuff is irrelevant;
Some small stuff is paramount;
Wisdom is knowing the difference.

4

"*M*aster," said the disciple, "I do not understand why my life feels so barren. You know that once I was a wastrel, but I have given up all those things. I put aside each day all those bad habits I once had, and yet I do not feel joy. Why?"

"You tend a garden, do you not?" asked the master.

"Yes," replied the disciple, "and I find joy in that."

"And you must know how to prune. Then consider," offered the master, "the difference between the plants you tend and bonsai. In both, the gardener prunes back unwanted or dead branches. You prune your plants to encourage healthy growth so they can bear fruit or flower, and you tend the soil so that the roots can grow strong and support growth. But in bonsai the roots are also pruned. When the roots don't grow, what happens to the plant?"

"Its growth is stunted," answered the disciple.

"Yes," continued the master. "In bonsai this is intentional and leads to an unnatural form. But what is pleasing in plants is not pleasing in people. You have pruned away the unwanted in your life, but you have spent all your energy in pruning and none in growing. Let your life grow in what is good. Be as diligent in growing as you are in pruning, and you will find joy."

The Hubble Space Telescope is a mega-project that developed a mega-problem. John G. Cramer, in "Mega-Projects & -Problems: the Hubble in Trouble" (*Analog Science Fiction/Science Fact*, February 1991), described the problem. Because of a slight aberration in the surface of the telescope's primary mirror, the image of a pointlike star became a bright spot surrounded by a bright "halo." This problem meant that only roughly 10% of the light collected could be delivered to the instrument packages aboard the craft. How "slight" was the aberration? About half of a wavelength of visible light.

Why wasn't the aberration detected earlier? It was—by a testing machine called a null-corrector used in the first phase of rough cutting of the mirror. But a more sophisticated null-corrector used later in the mirror's fabrication was itself flawed and didn't show the aberration. The difference in the two tests was attributed to the less sophisticated system and discounted. When the instruments that set the standard are flawed, the result can be disastrous.

Discipline—the training of the mental, moral, and physical powers by instruction, control, and exercise.

When leadership is flawed—when it does not measure up to high standards of integrity, ethics, and morality—the results can be equally disastrous. Effective leaders must check their character against those standards and, as needed, discipline themselves to come into alignment.

One reason for discipline is best described in the Bible: "I discipline my body so that I will not be disqualified" (1 Corinthians 9:25-27, paraphrased). That reason became very concrete for me several years ago when my family was preparing to leave for a month's vacation on the California coast.

I took our car to the local car wash to get it cleaned up for the trip. Before I went to the cashier I noticed some cassette tapes by the Beach Boys. I picked out two tapes and went to the cash register. The transaction took place and I walked outside to wait for my clean car. As I started to think about the amount of money I paid, I realized that I wasn't charged enough for the two tapes. The cashier rang up $.99 apiece instead of $4.99 apiece. I went back to the cashier and told her that she hadn't charged me enough money. I said, "I owe you another eight dollars plus tax." She looked at me and said, "I know you still owe me money. I was in your church last Sunday. I didn't charge you enough just to see if you were an honest man." Wow—my stomach jumped into my throat! She had been checking me out. I was very glad I was paying attention to the receipt, and I was certainly glad that I was committed to honesty.

Certainly no leader is perfect, but our world wants leaders who have integrity and honesty. High standards for effective leaders cannot be compromised.

Every church, every political structure, every enterprise private or public will never be any more disciplined than its leadership.

Therefore, for a leader, moral and ethical discipline is not optional—it is essential. An effective leader knows that his or her private life is a public matter. What leaders do in private shapes their habits. If their private lives are morally healthy, they will lead with morally healthy habits. If, privately, a leader compromises the highest Christian values, morals, and ethics, then that leader will self-destruct.

When I was a young pastor, Dr. Lloyd Ogilvie, senior pastor at Hollywood Presbyterian Church, told me that my church would never grow beyond the leadership. This helped me take leadership more seriously. As I reviewed the leadership of the church I was serving, I became very concerned. Some of the elected leaders came to church only once a month or less. Other leaders didn't give any money to the church. Still others were never involved in any mission programs. Yet they were expecting other people to do these things. I knew that people would not do what leaders were not willing to do themselves, so I began to take a serious look at leadership development.

I decided to offer leadership training seminars. After

these sessions, we all agreed that leadership required some standards of excellence in the private as well as the public life of every leader. This resulted in setting a "training schedule" for all of us that we still encourage our leaders to follow today:

1. Regular worship attendance
2. Daily devotions and prayer
3. Growth through participating in educational classes
4. Generous financial giving (10% of income) and investment of time and talents
5. Involvement in a mission project to the homeless or hungry, an orphanage or prison, or other opportunities of service

These commitments constantly need to be made and managed with grace. Certainly, these disciplines don't make God love anyone any more; nevertheless, striving to live by these standards assists every leader in becoming more effective.

The demands of leadership are great; however, the rewards of this disciplined kind of leadership are even greater. This kind of disciplined leadership had a part in leading a struggling, small church into an annual growth rate of 17%. Leaders who are themselves growing, produce growth. But it is more than numerical growth. Just as sick trees cannot produce healthy fruit, leaders who aren't growing don't inspire growth in others. But the opposite is also true—growing leaders inspire healthy mental, emotional, physical, and spiritual growth in others. Either there is growth, or there is decline. It depends upon the leadership.

Great leaders understand the importance of training. Training involves working very hard at the "small stuff" in life, as the theory on page 39 suggests. The things we take for granted can sometimes be the most difficult to achieve. Recently, I was golfing with a friend who confided to me how hard it was to live the Christian life. He said, "I try to be a Christian, but it's really hard."

Just as he finished his sentence a 747 airplane flew over our heads. I said to him, "How about going to the airport with me, and I'll try to fly a 747?" He laughed. I said, "We can no more try to fly that airplane than we can try to live the Christian life. *Trying* to live the Christian life is impossible. We have to *train* to live the Christian life."

In the Bible the importance of training is pointed out by the apostle Paul in 1 Corinthians:

> Do you not know that in a race all the runners run, but only one gets the prize? Run in such a way as to get the prize. Everyone who competes in the games goes into strict training. They do it to get a crown that will not last; but we do it to get a crown that will last forever. Therefore I do not run like a man running aimlessly; I do not fight like a man beating the air. No, I beat my body and make it my slave so that after I have preached to others, I myself will not be disqualified for the prize.
>
> 1 Corinthians 9:24-27 NIV

When I ran in the Fiesta Bowl marathon, I went into a training process. I started out training by running two miles a day. Then I increased over many months until I ran 26.2 miles. If I had not trained in this way, I would have collapsed and never finished the race. Leaders know that *training*, not simply trying, is the key to success.

Leadership workout

Practice determined discipline with these leadership toughness ideas:

Think positive thoughts.

Read the Bible daily.

Autograph each day with excellence.

Invite God's supernatural power to enter every part of your life.

Never quit—never, never, never quit.

Effective leadership requires loving unconditionally, envisioning the future exceptionally, affirming continually, disciplining with determination, and

ENERGIZING OTHERS ENTHUSIASTICALLY!

Chapter 5

Energize Others Enthusiastically

---

*An ounce of INSPIRATION
is worth a pound of PERSPIRATION.*

5

"A true leader must be like a ball," said the master, pointing to some children at play. "What do you observe about the ball's bounce?"

"Well," offered the disciple, "how high the ball bounces back depends on how hard the child throws it."

"So, for it to bounce higher, must it have more energy?" asked the master.

"Yes, the child must drop it from higher up, or throw it down harder."

"That is true of one ball alone," said the master, "but consider what would happen with two balls dropped together, one on top of the other."

The master walked over to the children and spoke to them. A little girl held out two balls side by side, then dropped them. From the same height, she then held one ball on top of the other and dropped them together. Laughing, she tried it again.

"Now what did you see?" the master asked.

"The top ball bounced higher than it did when dropped alone," replied the disciple.

"Yes, the ball below passed some of its energy on to the ball above, helping it to bounce higher. And so it is with people," observed the master. "Enthusiasm is the energy that, passed along, enables others to bounce higher."

The Buffalo Bills were playing the Houston Oilers in the first round of the Superbowl playoffs without their star quarterback, who was injured. By the end of the first half, the Bills were losing 35-3. But football history was about to be made.

In the second half, Frank Reich, the Bills' backup quarterback, energized himself and the team with enthusiasm, and passed for four touchdowns. The Bills won in overtime 41-38. It was called the greatest comeback in the history of the National Football League. The key to victory was Reich's enthusiastic inspiration.

Effective leaders have learned that their own enthusiasm sets off in other people a chain reaction of enthusiastic participation.

ENTHUSIASM:

lights a fire under the soul
creates energy
relieves boredom
helps us work with our whole heart

Effective leaders' hearts are filled to overflowing with contagious enthusiasm, which reveals their excitement toward, and commitment to, what needs to be accomplished. Enthusiasm builds enthusiasm in others and creates more positive interaction.

Effective leaders have learned that when a tough job needs to be done, doing it with enthusiasm may not make it easier, but will make it more enjoyable. All of us have had some "dirt-ball" jobs during our lives. The time when the complaining is the worst is the time a leader needs to be the most enthusiastic.

After Christmas we needed someone to take down all the Christmas decorations from the sanctuary and carefully put them away. Nobody wanted to do the job; many people grumbled and complained about being too tired to help out. On the Friday morning after the Christmas holidays, I used the telephone intercom on my desk to enthusiastically announce a "Christmas De-decoration Pizza Party" from 11:30 A.M. until 1:30 P.M. This enthusiastic offer received an enthusiastic response from my staff and, in less than two hours, the difficult job was done and the pizza consumed.

Enthusiasm helps us work with our whole heart. While visiting in Strasbourg, France, I was invited to a special six-course French dining experience. During the meal the head chef came out to introduce each new course. His enthusiasm was delightful. When we finished the delicious meal, he gave us his final words. He announced, "I enthusiastically prepare food. I always do it with my whole heart." His success was directly related to his enthusiasm. It is probably true that genuinely successful people are also enthusiastic people.

I saw a plaque in a shopping mall that contained the words of the great football coach Vince Lombardi on what it takes to be number one. The words on the plaque reflected the importance Lombardi placed on enthusiastic participation. I remember the plaque reading something like this: Every time a football player goes to ply his trade, he's got to play from the ground up—from the soles of his feet right up to his head. Every inch of him has to play. Some guys play with their heads. That's OK. You've got to be smart to be number one in any business. But more importantly, you've got to play with your heart, with every fiber of your body. If you're lucky enough to find a guy with a lot of head and a lot of heart, he's never going to come off the field second.

An effective leader knows that enthusiasm can't be faked. Phoney enthusiasm is negative and *demotivates* workers. The source of real enthusiasm is Jesus Christ. A Greek word for enthusiasm is *en-theos*, which means being full of God. When a leader is filled with God, he or she is full of authentic enthusiasm.

A Bible verse that fuels enthusiasm is "Trust in the Lord with all your heart and lean not on your own understanding; in all your ways acknowledge him, and he will make your paths straight" (Proverbs 3:5-6 NIV).

Leadership workout

Practice energizing others with enthusiasm with these suggestions:

1. Believe in their potential.

2. Teach them how to dream great dreams.

3. Point out their strengths.

4. Encourage them regularly by writing a note, making a phone call, or giving a gift.

So far we have seen that effective leaders: (1) love unconditionally, (2) envision the future exceptionally, (3) affirm continuously, (4) discipline with determination, and (5) energize others enthusiastically. Now we move on to see that the effective leader also

RISKS BOLDLY!

Chapter 6

Risk Boldly

---◆---

Risk isn't careless action—

Risk is "Faith in action"

6

*O*ne day as they were walking, the master and a disciple came to a place where a stream crossed the road. There was no bridge across the stream, but here the stream bed was rocky. "Let us rest for a while," suggested the master, and they sat in the shade of a tree and watched as other travelers crossed the stream.

From the shore to the center of the stream the rocks were plentiful, but from the center to the other side they were fewer and farther apart. The master and the disciple watched as travelers picked their way to the center, then hesitatingly stretched one leg to test their footing on the next rock. Often the stretch from rock to rock was too far, or the rocks were loose, and most travelers found themselves in the stream before reaching the other side. A few travelers, however, leaped from rock to rock seemingly with ease, and reached the other side completely dry.

"What does this tell you about faith?" the master asked the disciple.

"About faith? Why, nothing," answered the surprised disciple. "I should think that people who cross easily to the other side either know where the rocks are secure, or they have longer legs than those who slip and fall."

"Watch again," said the master. Three more travelers crossed the stream. The tallest swayed unsteadily and lurched and slipped into the water, as did his companion. The third crossed to the center, cautiously put out a foot to test several rocks, jumped quickly from one wobbly rock to the next, and leaped at last to the far side.

"Say," called the master to the third traveler, "you did that so easily; you must know which rocks won't wobble."

"Not at all," she called back. "I've never been this way before."

"Then how did you cross so easily?" asked the disciple.

"I trust my balance, not the rocks," the traveler laughed. "It's all in the jump. When you can't trust the rocks, sometimes both of your feet have to be in the air."

"Faith is knowing what to trust, then daring to jump," said the master.

Effective leaders are people of great faith. The essence of faith is risk. A leader constantly risks going where the possibility of failure is greater than the possibility of success.

The movie *Columbus 1492* contained a great line for leaders. Columbus had a nautical map for the journey; however, he and his crew sailed beyond the map. They sent a message back to headquarters with the report, "We have sailed beyond the map; please send further instructions."

LEADERS ARE ALWAYS GOING OFF THE MAP

Robert Schuller has said that it takes guts to leave the ruts. An effective leader chooses to leave the ruts: ruts of routine, ruts of status quo, ruts of maintaining mediocrity. However, to leave the ruts for new routes, new ways, new ideas, new methods, new styles, and new structures is risky.

Recently our congregation voted unanimously to leave everything we have and relocate our church to a site several miles away. This relocation is very risky. Lyle Schaller, a wise church consultant, told me to be careful throughout the relocation process. He compared it to a winter in the North. Early in winter the lakes freeze over, but it can be dangerous to walk across them because ice doesn't freeze to the same depth all over the lake. There are often places of thin ice. In fact, he warned that in relocating, the possibility of failure was greater than the possibility of success. Yet we are willing to lay everything on the line because the move has to be made. Without more room to grow, our mission will stop growing. When growth stops, death begins.

Leaders become trailblazers; they go where no one has gone before and do what no one has done before.

Effective leadership is like walking on a frozen lake. There are places where the ice is pretty thin. That is where faith goes into action. Faith believes that God will find a way; if you fall through into the icy water, God is able even then to rescue and restore you. It isn't always easy to decide when it is good to take a risk and when it is foolish. Studying all sides of an issue and listening for God's direction help make the decision.

In Lloyd Ogilvie's book, *Falling Into Greatness* (Thomas Nelson Publishing, 1984), he relates this story:

A friend of mine, a high flier in the circus in his youth, tells me that the secret of becoming a successful trapeze artist is in overcoming the fear of falling.

"Once you know that the net below will catch you, you stop worrying about falling," he says. "You actually learn to fall successfully! What I mean is, you can concentrate on catching the trapeze swinging toward you, and not on falling, because repeated falls in the past have convinced you that the net is strong and reliable when you do fall. The rope in the net hurts only if you stiffen up and resist it. The result of falling and being caught by the net is a mysterious confidence and daring on the trapeze. You fall less. Each fall makes you able to risk more!"

I love the anecdote of the skier who accidentally misses a turn and ends up careering over the edge of a mountain cliff. Halfway down the mountain he lunges for a tree branch sticking out of the side of the mountain. He is able to grab hold of the branch to stop his fall. As he is hanging there, he looks up and then down. He realizes he can't get up and, if he lets go, he will certainly tragically fall to the bottom. In his desperation he looks toward heaven and yells, "Is anybody up there?"

Out of heaven comes a booming voice, "Yes, I'm up here."

Relieved, the skier yells, "Can you help me?"

The voice booms back, "Yes, I can help you. All you have to do is let go of the branch. Just trust me."

Clinging tightly to the branch, the skier looks down to the bottom of the mountain. Then he looks back up, and with a terrified scream says, "Is anybody else up there?"

Letting go is hard to do, but a white-knuckled grip on the present isn't a choice for a leader. Effective leadership is willing to take the risks necessary to accomplish the mission that God has destined for those who trust and believe. The essence of faith is risk.

Confident optimism based on God's faithfulness produces tremendous results.

Leadership workout

Make a practical application of risking boldly by doing the following:

Reach beyond your own comfort zone.

Invite Jesus Christ to fill you with mountain-moving faith.

Search for bold and daring opportunities to put faith to work.

Keep confident that with God all things are possible.

Let's review the leadership principles represented by the letters in *LEADER*. An effective leader

L—Loves unconditionally
E—Envisions the future exceptionally
A—Affirms continuously
D—Disciplines with determination
E—Energizes others enthusiastically
R—Risks boldly, and

SERVES SELFLESSLY!

Chapter 7

Serve Selflessly

———◆———

Out of Service—out of order, ineffective, broken, not functioning properly

In Service—in proper order, effective, whole, functioning as it should

A LEADER SHOULD ALWAYS BE "IN SERVICE"

7

"*A* true leader," said the master, "must have a servant's heart. Two experienced pilots prepared for a flight. The first pilot sat in the cockpit saying to herself, 'I am a pilot. My job is to fly, not to be a mechanic.' She asked the ground crew to double-check the flaps, rudder, landing gear, and fuel tanks. She delegated to her copilot the job of checking the brakes and controls, filing the flight plan, and checking the weather. When the crew had finished, the pilot got clearance from the tower and took off.

"The second pilot said to himself, 'The lives of these people and the safety of this aircraft are in my hands.' He himself checked the brakes and controls. He walked all around the aircraft, checking the flaps, rudder, landing gear, and fuel tanks. He filed the flight plan and checked the weather. After double-checking with the crew to see that they had carried out their duties, the second pilot got clearance from the tower and took off.

"Now with which pilot," asked the master, "would you rather fly?"

"With the second," came the disciple's unhesitating reply. "He took personally his responsibility to the aircraft and the crew."

"And who was truly in command?" asked the master.

"The second pilot," answered the disciple, "because he had a servant's heart."

Effective leaders don't see themselves as celebrities to be served; rather, they see themselves as servants who are eager to serve. United States Senator John McCain is a friend of mine. He has often asked how he could help me. When we are together, he sincerely wants to know what he can do for me. He is a leader with a servant's heart.

Cindy McCain is the spouse of the senator. She has organized medical teams that travel to the most devastated and helpless countries of the world. Because of her servant leadership, she received one of our world's most prestigious honors, the Citizen of the World Award. I was with Cindy as she received the award. At that gala event I spent some time with Dr. Henry Kissinger. During our time together I told him a humorous story I had heard about him.

I began: "The story's told about the time Dr. Kissinger, the president of the United States, a priest, a hippie, and a pilot were flying together. Suddenly the plane's engines malfunctioned. The pilot announced that the plane was destined to crash. After giving the bad news, he added that, after checking out the safety equipment, he found only four parachutes for the five people. Since the airplane was his, the first parachute was also his. Following the pilot's jump, the president informed the others that the next parachute was his because the country really needed him. Next Dr. Kissinger told the priest and the hippie that, because he was the smartest man in the world, he needed to live. He reached out and grabbed the next pack and jumped. The priest turned to the hippie and urged him to take the last parachute, saying that he had had a great life and was ready to meet God. The hippie replied, 'Hey, Father, don't worry, because the smartest man in the world just grabbed my backpack!'"

When I told Dr. Kissinger the story, he didn't crack a smile. Pausing a moment, he responded that he was pretty smart. So smart, in fact, that when he gave a bad speech, people thought it was their fault. We enjoyed a good laugh together.

That night, Dr. Kissinger told how John McCain's father had been in charge of all the troops during the pinnacle of the Vietnam War. His son, John, had been taken prisoner and was held in an unknown camp. As the war escalated, John's father had to order a bombing raid, not knowing whether the raid would sacrifice his son or not. Of course John McCain made it out alive, but John's father clearly demonstrated selfless leadership.

God led with selfless service giving his one and only son to be sacrificed on a cross so that the world could be saved. That giving, sacrificial servant leadership is what it will take to effectively lead our world into the 21st century and beyond.

Jesus himself did not come to be served, but to serve. God gives the clear message that those who want to have the greatest influence and most significant impact must be servants of all. Effective leaders always seek selfless servanthood by finding needs and meeting them, by finding problems and solving them, and by finding hurts and healing them.

When President John Kennedy presented his blueprint for effective leadership, he told Americans to ask not what their country could do for them, but rather to ask what they could do for their country. Effective leaders do not seek what others can do for them, but rather what they can do for others.

I am inspired by the people around me who serve so selflessly. Police officer Dave Logan is one of those people. His life was changed in the split second of a gunshot. On Dave's last shift before his scheduled vacation, an attacker's bullet ripped his larynx and esophagus and partially severed his spinal cord, paralyzing him from the neck down. As Dave conquered the odds, he came to realize that it was a miracle of God that he even survived.

Out of a thankful heart and a commitment to walk out of the hospital, Dave amazed everyone. When most people would have quit, Dave didn't. There were moments of unbearable pain and suffering. However, today Dave has committed himself to serve selflessly. He is active serving in our church's care ministry. Dave goes to schools and helps young people decide not to do drugs. Selfless serving has brought Dave significant satisfaction.

There is also Linda's story. She came into my office on December 24, 1989. Through her tears she shared her sad story. She had no money, no food, and no presents for her two children. After a couple of phone calls, I arranged for a family to adopt her family for Christmas. Her Christmas was transformed from tragedy to triumph.

The next Christmas, Linda came back to me and asked if she could adopt some families that were facing the crisis she faced a year earlier. I arranged for her to adopt a couple of families. Then the next year Linda got more people involved in a Christmas "Angel Tree" project. For Christmas 1993, Linda led our entire church and community in helping 5,000 children. Serving selflessly can have amazing results.

Leadership workout

Practice improving your service with these suggestions:

1. Find a need and fill it today.

2. Find a hurt and heal it today.

3. Find a problem and solve it today.

4. Find a hungry mouth and feed it today.

5. Find a person needing clothes and clothe her or him today.

Once more, effective leadership:

L—Loves unconditionally
E—Envisions the future exceptionally
A—Affirms continuously
D—Disciplines with determination
E—Energizes others enthusiastically
R—Risks boldly
S—Serves selflessly

and

HOPES RELENTLESSLY!

Chapter 8

Hope Relentlessly

---

*Those who HOPE
are
those who can COPE.*

8

One day the master and a disciple sat on a hillside. The slopes were covered with the fine, pale green of new grass pushing through the earth. The master plucked a slender shoot from the ground.

"What," the master asked, "is as powerful as the tiny tip of this grass seedling? If the tip is cut off, the seedling's growth will slow and, eventually, stop. But if the tip is replaced on the stem, the seedling will begin to grow again."

"What is it in the tip that can be so powerful?" asked the disciple.

"A substance called auxin," replied the master. "It is so powerful that one drop, even diluted a million times, can produce measurable growth. One tiny ounce could produce enough plant growth in this area of grass that the stems of the blades of grass, laid end to end, could encircle the earth.

"You have something that powerful within you," the master continued, "and that something is hope. If one tiny ounce of auxin could produce so much new growth, what could one tiny ounce of hope do within you?"

The Swiss theologian Emil Brunner is credited with having said, "What oxygen is to the lungs, such is hope to

the meaning of life." We cannot endure without hope.
Hope is more than optimism; hope is more than getting
what we want. Hope is believing in the dawn when the
darkness covers us.

There is a famous story of hope and faith that you
may have heard. In 17th-century England, public worship
was considered a crime. Thousands of churches were torn
down and demolished. One man in that climate dared to
build a church. It was a church built on the hope in his
heart that a better day was coming. The church still
stands in England. There is an inscription over the door
that reads:

In the Year 1653, when all things sacred
throughout the nation were either
demolished or profaned, Sir Robert Shirley
founded this church, whose singular praise
it is to have done the best of things in the
worst of times and hoped them in the most
calamitous.

Effective leaders *hope relentlessly* because they know
that, when everything has been tried, and you are at the
end of your rope—you simply tie a knot and hang on. A
leader knows that *to hope is to be able to cope.* The Bible
puts it this way:

We know that suffering produces perseverance; perseverance, character; and character,
hope. And hope does not disappoint us, because
God has poured out his love into our hearts by
the Holy Spirit, whom he has given us.

Romans 5:3-5 NIV

This hope isn't based on wishful optimism; rather, it
is founded on the certainty of God's faithfulness. Relentless hope is confident that God is always way ahead of us,

already into the future, arranging the best and maximizing all of the possibilities.

Relentless hope transforms "I've got to see it to believe it" into "I've got to believe to see it."

Relentless hope trusts God wholeheartedly. Community Church of Joy demonstrated relentless hope when, in May of 1992, with no money in hand and knowing that the possibility of failure was greater than the possibility of success, we made the commitment to relocate on a 127-acre orange grove five miles away. The first "hope test" came the next year on May 15, when we found ourselves $125,000 short of a $750,000 down payment. The owner of the land agreed to an extension. Three months later we were still praying and hoping for the funds to arrive. Our hope was in the reality that, what God decides, God provides. Not only were we confident that the $125,000 would arrive; we were confident that the entire $3,200,000 to purchase the land would come in. And indeed it did. Eight months later we had exceeded our goal with a total of four million dollars. Even if the purchase is delayed, and leadership gets anxious, God won't be anxious, because God's hope never disappoints us.

Hope based on God's faithfulness produces tremendous encouragement. At a recent board meeting we began with each person sharing a personal need that we could pray about for one another. The number one need was for encouragement. As we prayed for encouragement, we sensed a renewed spirit of hope. This hope gave us new energy to accomplish the challenging work ahead of us.

Relentless hope creates energy. A work environment saturated with hope is energetic and effective. There is nothing more draining than hopelessness. A hopeless environment generates low morale, poor productivity, and depression. An effective leader knows that an attitude of *"What's the use?"* causes dis-ease, dejection, and despair. On the other hand, an attitude of *"Nothing is impossible with God"* produces health, vitality, and joy.

Great leaders model hope. They know that hope is more *caught* than *taught*. Little three-year-old Sara Johnson's heart barely quivered for eight straight days. Her mom and dad didn't give up hope of getting a transplanted heart that could change everything. In another hospital four-year-old Tara Anderson was about to die from a ruptured artery in her brain that left her brain-dead. Tara's mom and dad donated Tara's heart to Sara. Sara received Tara's heart, but five days later the two little girls who had shared a heart now shared heaven together.

The story doesn't end there. A short time later, Sara's mother, Paula, found out that she had cancer. Not long after that she discovered that she was pregnant. Even though she was advised by her doctors to abort the child because of the serious cancer treatments needed, Paula didn't lose hope that she would live to give birth to a healthy child. She was right! Nine months later a healthy little baby was born.

On Thanksgiving Day in 1993 the Andersons and the Johnsons joined in the celebration as I baptized that new little miracle child. Certainly Sara and Tara can never be replaced; nevertheless, there was a great joy celebrated on Thanksgiving Day. That joy was sustained by the hope and faith in God of the family and friends.

Another example of hope is the story of Dennis Byrd. Doctors gave New York Jets defensive end Dennis Byrd little hope. A paralyzing collision with a teammate in a November 1992 football game with the Kansas City Chiefs left Dennis with a spinal cord shattered in three places. The prognosis was that he probably would never walk again. Doctors warned that it would be two years after his surgery before they could know for certain. Despite the dire predictions, Dennis and his wife Angela believed he would walk again. When, three days after surgery, Dennis struggled to move his toes and succeeded, it confirmed for them that what they believed would, indeed, become reality.

Dennis sent a message through Angela to all those waiting for word of his condition. Her message was, "Dennis says he's glad God chose him for this, because he has the strength to handle it." And they had the hope to handle it; through every hard-fought, tiny victory, Dennis and

Angela believed. From bed to wheelchair, through difficult therapy, from wheelchair to crutches, on February 12, 1993, Dennis Byrd walked out of the hospital. Dennis and Angela Byrd are models of hope.

An effective leader is convinced that the imprints of hope are essential. There is a painting of a blindfolded woman with her head bowed, holding a lyre and sitting on a globe. The lyre has only one string unbroken, and only one star shines in the sky. A one-word description hangs underneath the picture—*HOPE*.

An effective leader knows that, when the last light is about to go out, and the last string is frayed and ready to break, there is still reason to hope. As my father was about to die after a valiant battle with cancer, he communicated the power of hope in these words: *Your future is as bright as the promise of God.* The Bible puts it in these words: " 'For I know the plans I have for you,' declares the Lord, 'plans to prosper you and not to harm you, plans to give you hope and a future' " (Jeremiah 29:11 NIV).

Leadership workout

Practice relentless hope with these suggestions:

Hang on to every promise God ever made.

Offer yourself fully to God's care and keeping.

Plan for a fantastic future.

Eagerly wait for God's reward.

The Bible tells us, "Those who hope in the Lord will renew their strength. They will soar on wings like eagles; they will run and not grow weary, they will walk and not be faint" (Isaiah 40:31 NIV).

Hope fires the imagination so that a leader can

IMAGINE IMMEASURABLY!

Chapter 9

Imagine Immeasurably

———◆———

*If life is a fire,
FAITH is the fuel,
but
IMAGINATION is the spark
that ignites it.*

9

*T*he master and a disciple sat on a hill a short distance outside the city, watching the stars. "What a long way off they are," the disciple remarked. "They make me wonder what's out there. They make me think of the future, too," she went on. "How can we possibly imagine what lies ahead?"

"Let's imagine," said the master, "that you want to go back to the car. Will you take a candle to find your way?"

"Well, I could, but I'd rather use a flashlight," the disciple replied.

"Why?" asked the master.

"I'd have to walk very slowly with a candle, because a candle casts a weak light. It couldn't light enough of the way ahead. A flashlight would be more sensible; it illuminates more," she said.

"And when you drive back home, will you use a flashlight to light the road?" the master continued.

"No," answered the disciple. "That won't work; a flashlight isn't strong enough to light the road as far ahead as I need to see in order to drive safely."

"So you'll need a light with a longer beam," said the master. "Imagination is like a light; it can illuminate much or little, depending on where you want to go. Your beam—your dream—should be long enough to match your journey."

An effective leader knows that imagination is one of God's greatest gifts to us. When our imagination is active, there are amazing results. Effective leaders know the incredible worth of the imagination.

As a little boy, I remember adults telling us children that we had wild imaginations. Whenever a grade school classmate would be lost in his or her imagination, we were told to stop that "silly daydreaming." Imagination didn't seem to be encouraged or valued as much as intelligence. Yet without our imaginations, this world would be dull, routine, and stagnant.

This was written and given to me by a friend, Lolly Pisoni, a dynamic leader who always imagines immeasurably:

Dare to dream

When you wish upon a star
Makes no difference who you are ...
Your dreams come true.

Childhood is a magical time
  regardless of whether you grew up in a happy or
  unhappy family.
You really believe wishing on a star makes wishes
  come true,
so ... you dare to dream!

But somewhere along the way we learn that all
  dreams do not come true and there is no Jiminy
  Cricket.
We experience disappointment, and we may begin to
  feel that dreaming is a waste of time and effort.

In our quest to fulfill our wishes in another way as
  we grow up,
we learn to be competent—to know all there is to
  know and always be right. In doing this we lose the
  natural curiosity and wonder of childhood.

Dare to dream like a child
and
    plan like an adult.

Clearly God has an incredible imagination. Every day a new baby, a priceless original, is born. Everyone is created in the image of God; yet how amazing it is that every person has one-of-a-kind fingerprints and features. Imagine creating billions of people with no copies! That kind of imagination has been given to us as an inheritance from God.

Imagination is the instigator of inventions—tools, machinery, vehicles, devices to communicate, medicine—and the list goes on. Imagination leads you to investigate the unknown. It helps you consider and respect new ideas.

How can leaders make the most of their imagination? The first step is to *treasure* it. Imagination is one of our greatest assets. It needs to always be treated as a priceless part of life. Even if every material possession in the world is lost, with imagination we can rise up and rebuild. A leader knows the only people truly bankrupt are the ones who have lost their imagination.

The second step in making the most of our imagination is to *test* it. I can say from personal experience that imagination testing can end in success, but it can also end in failure. When our imagination test is successful, it is rewarding. A current imagination test for me and Community Church of Joy is the acquiring of 127 acres of land for our church's relocation and expansion. As this project is developing, my imagination is being tested immeasurably.

When imagination testing leads to failure, what do leaders do? Truthfully, imagination failure is more frequent than success. Not long after I arrived as pastor at Community Church of Joy, some people had decided that the changes stemming from my imagination and my desire to connect with the nonreligious people of the community were not acceptable. One of the changes that was upsetting to many people was changing a few of the traditional worshiping methods. Even though I continued the one traditional worship service Joy had always offered and simply added a contemporary worship celebration, it was resisted. I was told that two worship services would split the church. People began to question my worth as a pastor. As a result of this and other problems, nearly one-half of the 252 members left the church. Everything seemed to be going wrong. I really felt like a failure. But this feeling of failure, like every failure, sharpened my imagination. I am reminded of Thomas Edison, the great inventor, who failed thousands of times experimenting with his imagination. Leaders often learn more from failure than from success. Failure can be a great friend of every imagination.

Step three in making the most of our imagination is to *trust* it. We are often afraid to take this third step because we never want to look foolish. When our imagination produces something that has never been done or even thought of before, the tendency is to play it safe to avoid the possibility of being misunderstood or laughed at.

A few years ago, during my doctoral studies, I saw a crowd waiting for hours to get into a movie theater to see *Batman.* My imagination kicked in, imagining what it would take to have crowds of people waiting to get into church Sunday after Sunday. At that moment the idea of "entertainment evangelism" entered my mind. As a result, I wrote an article and submitted it for publication. After the article was published, I received hundreds of letters— of support, as well as outright rage. This stimulated more conversation about evangelism than I had ever heard before. Trusting my imagination had a positive result.

Effective leaders know that imagination adds value to life and needs to be encouraged. God made us a fantastic promise that can keep our imagination brilliantly burning for a lifetime: "No eye has seen, no ear has heard, no mind has conceived what God has prepared for those who love him" (1 Corinthians 2:9 NIV).

Leadership workout

Increase your power of imagination with these suggestions:

Investigate the unknown.

Make friends with creative thinkers.

Accept daydreaming as a productive time, not a waste of time.

Give great respect to new ideas.

Invite difficulty, because difficulty provides grist for the imagination mill.

Notice God's imaginative creation.

Eye imagining with the "eye of the tiger"—go for it.

IMAGINATION
HOPE
SERVICE
RISK
ENTHUSIASM
DISCIPLINE
AFFIRMATION
ENVISIONING and
LOVE

are essential for effective leadership. However, without persistent prayer, effective leadership is impossible. Great leaders

PRAY PERSISTENTLY!

Chapter 10

Pray Persistently

———◆———

PERSISTENT PRAYER
produces
PERSISTENT POWER

10

"*M*aster," cried the disciple, "I so often grow weary. I see all that needs to be done, but I am only one person. I want to do more, but how can I? Where can I find rest, and how can I find the strength to go on when the task is so great?"

"Walk with me," replied the master, and he led the disciple to a pool that fed a small stream. Beside the stream stood a smithy, from which came the huff of bellows and the ringing of hammers. Outside the shop stood barrels of nails, and hung from the walls were racks of finished utensils, hinges, and horseshoes. A blacksmith came outside carrying a newly made hook.

"This is a busy shop," commented the disciple. "You must have several smiths working here."

"Come inside," laughed the blacksmith, and they followed him into the noisy shop. To his amazement, the disciple saw no one else there. But the bellows puffed and the noise of two hammers still rang out, driven by strong rods all connected to a single shaft. Turning the shaft was one mighty beam moving back and forth constantly.

"I'm the only one," the smith answered. Seeing the disciple's puzzled look he went on explaining. "The beam is driven by a mill wheel outside. The pool is fed by an underground spring which flows year round, and a race channels water from the pool to the wheel. I have all the help I need every day from the spring."

The master and the disciple went back outside and stood at the edge of the pool. "The smith built the race, the wheel, and the beam to connect his work with the power of the spring. God, like the spring, is the source of your power. Through prayer you build the race, the wheel, and the beam to connect your work to the ever-flowing power of God. Through prayer you will find your strength and your renewal."

———————◆———————

On a brilliant Sunday morning in Canberra, Australia, I was telling a story about two parrots. Whenever anyone would come in the door of my friend's house, his parrot would squawk, "I want a kiss; I want a kiss." This startled and shocked many of his guests, so I decided to fix the problem.

I brought my *honorable* parrot to my friend's house to teach his parrot how to act. My thought was that my parrot had an excellent opportunity to be a positive witness because it spent most of each day with its wings folded calling out, "I want to pray; I want to pray."

As expected, as soon as I walked in the door, my friend's parrot blurted out, "I want a kiss; I want a kiss." Suddenly my parrot started acting strangely. His eyes bulged out. He started to vigorously flap his wings, and he screamed, "My prayers are answered; my prayers are answered."

When I finished the story, to the surprise of all that were gathered there, two parrots were perched in the window right beside me. We all had a good laugh.

I use this humorous story to make the point that prayer does work.

Effective leaders know that nothing great ever happens without prayer. Persistent prayer keeps a leader plugged into the greatest power in all the world—God. PRAYER WORKS!

I admit that, up until four or five years ago, my prayer life was wimpy. Prayer got crowded out by my hectic lifestyle. Certainly I would find a few minutes every day for purposeful prayer, but my prayer practice was the opposite of Martin Luther's. When Luther, the great leader of the Reformation, got busy, he prayed more. When I got busy, I prayed less.

There is a story that once Luther faced a particularly difficult, demanding day, so he got up earlier in order to spend a few more hours in prayer. He understood the relationship between prayer and endurance. What an important example Martin Luther has been to me. As my life has gotten more demanding, my prayer life has taken on greater priority.

One of the helpful prayer tools making that happen has been prayer journaling. Every morning as I journal, I am more aware that prayer works wonders. One of the rewards of prayer journaling has been celebrating all the answered prayers. Another benefit is being able to keep my promise when I tell someone that I will remember to pray for him or her. It often bothered me when I promised someone I'd pray for them, and, after a couple of days, I'd forget. Now when I promise to pray, I write it down and can persistently pray.

It has been remarkable at Community Church of Joy to see that, as the leaders grow in intentional, persistent prayer, the church has grown both in numbers and in maturity. One of the best decisions made was to hire a full-time pastor of prayer. His leadership in prayer has led to 2,000 people per week actively participating in the prayer ministry. Last year nearly 50,000 people from around the world participated in Joy's prayer network.

God made it very clear that there is a crucial relationship between prayer and effective leadership. The greatest leader who ever lived, Jesus Christ, said that whatever we ask for in prayer, we will receive. Now that's a powerful promise. Jesus prayed persistently, sometimes throughout the entire night. His leadership demonstrated the power and priority of prayer. Jesus was teaching us through his own prayer practice and habits that prayer connects us with God's own thoughts and feelings. This provides every leader with greater wisdom, discernment, understanding, insight, encouragement, confidence, and courage.

Prayer also helps put problems into perspective. Prayer reminds us that we don't need to run to God to say how big our *problem* is; rather, we need to run to our problem and tell it how big *God* is. When we can do that, we are convinced that there is no problem as big as God. This is a critical step in a leader's effectiveness.

The effective leader is convinced that prayer is *transformational*. Significant transformation is powerfully illustrated in the following poem.

The Touch of the Master's Hand

'Twas battered and scarred, and the auctioneer
    thought it was hardly worth his while
To waste much time with the old violin,
But he held it up with a smile.
"Give me a dollar, and who'll make it two?
Only two dollars, who'll make it three?
Three dollars twice, and that's a good price,
But who's got a bid for me?"
The air was hot and the people just
Stood there as the sun was setting low.
Then from the back of the crowd a gray-haired man
Came forward and picked up the bow.
He wiped the dust from the old violin,
And he tightened up the strings.
Then he played out a melody, pure and sweet,
Sweet as the angels sing.
The music ended, and the auctioneer,
With a voice that was quiet and low,
Said "What is my bid for the old violin?"

And he held it up with the bow.
"A thousand dollars, and who'll make it two?
Only two thousand, and who'll make it three?
Three thousand twice, and that's a good price,
But who's got a bid for me?"
And the people called out, "What made the change?
We don't understand."
The auctioneer stopped and said with a smile,
"It was the touch of the master's hand."

Now many a person with their life out of tune
Is battered and scarred with sin.
And they're auctioned cheap to a broken world,
Much like the old violin.
But then the Master comes and the foolish crowd,
They never understand
The worth of a soul or the change that is brought
By the touch of the Master's hand.

Poet unknown

Leadership workout

Practice praying persistently with these suggestions:

Program yourself to make prayer a way of life. Try praying whenever you hear a siren or when you pass a homeless person or see a neighbor.

Record prayer requests and answers. This will provide evidence of how powerfully prayer works.

Accelerate prayer time when you accelerate your schedule.

Yield prime time and energy to making prayer a priority.

My prayer is that, as leaders, we can provide the effective leadership our world needs—to be put in touch, and stay in touch, with the Master Leader—Jesus Christ!

Postscript

Two years after I finished college I considered becoming an ordained minister, but I was never really sure that I wanted to experience the difficulties my father had as a pastor. When I'd mention the idea to my wife, she would quietly set aside whatever she was doing, look at me, and say, "Shut up!" She never wanted to marry a minister and she was sure that the last thing I should do was become an ordained clergyman.

In 1973 I met with Dr. Alvin Rogness, then the president of Luther Seminary, to ask him if he thought I should become an ordained pastor. His response was that if I could possibly stay away from the seminary, I shouldn't come. However, if I sensed God's call so irresistibly that I couldn't stay away, then I needed to enroll.

God's irresistible call to full-time ordained ministry came in 1975. By the way, God was really good to me, for my wife sensed the same calling for me. During my seminary days I dreamed about a visionary, loving, caring, mission-oriented church. My greatest hope was that people would see the church as a place that outgives, outshares, outloves, and outdares for the sake of Jesus Christ.

My excitement continued to grow as I received my first call to a 252-member congregation, Community Church of Joy, in Glendale, Arizona. On June 1, 1978, I enthusiastically began my work as the pastor of CCOJ. Over the next several months my enthusiasm waned. There was much turmoil within the church, and it soon was tearing me apart. To make matters worse, some members were secretly trying to figure out a good way to get rid of me. Some people had decided that my enthusiasm for the changes essential to connect with nonreligious people was not acceptable. On top of everything, church membership was rapidly declining.

If anything excellent and effective was going to happen at CCOJ, God was going to have to do it. I recall placing my life, my failures, and my future ministry into God's hands. I prayed that God would fill me with new hope and new love.

A number of events over the next two years, including a church fire and a new fire within me, brought change to CCOJ. Gradually the church grew, and it has been growing ever since. We discovered that everything we need for life abundant and life eternal is available to us in the gospel of Jesus Christ. We committed ourselves to bringing the good news of the gospel to nonreligious, unchurched people in our community. We celebrate our tradition, and we blend it with new methods, new styles, new structure, new music, new models, and new strategies to bring God's Word into the lives of all people in a meaningful way.

—Walt Kallestad

Community Church of Joy in Glendale, Arizona, is dedicated to helping others understand what it means to be a purpose-driven church and to effectively share the gospel with the unchurched. One excellent resource available to you is CCOJ's annual conference, "Reaching the Unchurched: New Evangelism Models for Mainline Congregations." For more information contact CCOJ at (602) 938-1460.

Augsburg Fortress Publishers provides a full line of resources for individuals and congregations, including books, curriculum, music, computer software, ecclesiastical arts, and general products. For more information about resources, check with your local Christian bookstore or regional Augsburg Fortress branch.